Christmas

BY
Jane Duden

CRESTWOOD HOUSE
New York

BUCHANAN DISTRICT LIBRARY

Library of Congress Cataloging-in-Publication Data
Duden, Jane.
  Christmas.

  p.   cm.—(Holidays)
  Includes bibliographical references.
  Summary: Explores the customs, traditions, symbols, and trivia of
Christmas and how the holiday is celebrated around the world.
  1. Christmas—Juvenile literature. (1. Christmas.) I. Title. II. Series: Holidays (New York, N.Y.)
GT4985.5.D83   1990   394.2'68282 — dc20   89-28520   CIP
ISBN 0-89686-497-9   AC

Photo Credits
Cover: Devaney Stock Photos
Culver Pictures, Inc.: 4, 17, 21, 29, 30, 32, 40, 43
Journalism Services: (Rick Bamman) 7; 18
DRK Photo: (D. Cavagnaro) 9; (Randy Trine) 10; (D. Krasemann) 12
Devaney Stock Photos: 22,25,26
Berg & Associates: (Kirk Schlea) 35; (Len Berger) 37

Copyright © 1990 by Crestwood House, Macmillan Publishing Company

Macmillan Publishing Company
866 Third Avenue
New York, NY 10022
Collier Macmillan Canada, Inc.

Printed in the United States

First Edition

10 9 8 7 6 5 4 3 2 1

Contents

Holiday or holy day – whichever way you view it – Christmas is the happiest and busiest time of year for millions of people.

Does Christmas make you think of home and family? Or fancy cookies, school vacations, and gifts under the Christmas tree? Celebrating traditions that have been handed down over the years is a big part of holiday fun. Christmas is impossible to ignore, as Scrooge once tried to do. And it is impossible not to catch the spirit!

The Most Celebrated Holiday

Winter festivals have been celebrated from the earliest days of recorded history. When Christmas began nearly 2,000 years ago, it borrowed from the earlier winter festivals. Today, throughout the world, Christmas is observed in one form or another. Each new culture has added its own customs and traditions to the old. Christmas has become the most celebrated holiday in the world.

Christmas is celebrated in different ways around the world. Here children in 19th-century Germany decorate their tree on Christmas morning.

The Birth of a Child

Christmas is the Christian holiday that celebrates the birth of Jesus Christ. The name is formed from "Christ" and "mass," the Sunday church service. Christians believe Jesus is the Son of God. The 2,000-year-old story is found in the Bible. An angel told a young woman named Mary that she had been chosen by God to be the mother of Jesus. When it was almost time for the birth, Mary and her husband, Joseph, traveled to Bethlehem to register for taxes. While they were there, the time came for the baby to be born. Because there was no room for Mary and Joseph in the inn, the baby Jesus was born in a stable.

The Gospels in the Bible tell of miraculous events at the time of Jesus' birth. The Gospel of Luke describes how an angel from God appeared to shepherds. The Gospel of Matthew tells how the Wise Men (called the Magi) followed a bright star to the place in Bethlehem where Jesus was born. They brought gifts and worshiped the child. The story of these events is called the Nativity. The birth of Jesus was the beginning of the Christian religion and the reason for celebrating Christmas.

No one knows the exact day and year of Christ's birth. The Gospels give no certain clues. We know that Jesus was born in Bethlehem of Judea while Herod was the king. Few records of birth were kept in those days. Astronomers, religious experts, and historians still argue about the most probable year of Christ's birth.

The most recent studies say Christ was born in the year 8 B.C. In A.D. 336, December 25 was mentioned as the date of Christmas on the Roman calendar. During the late 300s, Christianity became the official religion of the Roman Empire. The powerful Romans ruled many countries. Each country was made up of many different cul-

Teenagers reenact the birth of Christ in a stable with real livestock.

tures and religions, but the Romans wanted to convert everyone to their religion, Christianity. They wanted people to follow the teachings of their Christian church. Though no one was certain of Jesus' birthday, Christian leaders chose December 25 to represent it. They were influenced by the celebrations that had taken place for centuries before Jesus' birth.

Ancient Winter Festivals

At first, only a small number of people in the Roman Empire were Christians. All the non-Christians were called *pagans*. The pagans had festivals of their own on or near December 25. For example, Romans held year-end celebrations to honor Mithras, their god of light.

One of the most popular pagan festivals was Saturnalia. This harvest festival was celebrated with games, masks, and parades. People gave gifts to each other and prepared special foods. They decorated their homes with green branches. Everywhere, people stopped work to join in the celebration.

Other pagan year-end festivals celebrated the rebirth of the sun. Today, we know the shorter daylight hours of winter are caused by earth's path around the sun. But in ancient times when the days got shorter, people were afraid the sun might go away for good. The sun was important. It meant light and heat. The sun made the crops grow. When the days got shorter and the sun started to go away, people had celebrations to lure it back. The winter solstice takes place on or about December 21. That is when the earth is farthest from the sun. People brought greens into their homes to symbolize the green of spring that would return with the sun. They eventually understood the colder, shorter days of winter would gradually turn into the longer, warmer days of spring. They held great fires, feasts, and merrymaking to celebrate the rebirth of the sun.

Christian leaders did not have an easy time converting non-Christians, or pagans, to the Christian religion. Pagans liked their harvest and winter festivities. They did not want to give them up. That is why, over the years, popes (the spiritual rulers of the Roman Catholic church) and church leaders allowed many favorite ancient customs to become part of Christmas celebrations.

Winter festivals used to celebrate the time when the short, dark days of winter began to turn into the warmer, longer days of spring.

Many Christmas symbols have their roots more in pagan customs than in the story of Christ. The use of Christmas trees and other greenery and candles and other lights to decorate homes comes from pagan celebrations. In Italy, France, and Spain, fireworks on Christmas are common. French settlers in the 1700s brought the custom to Louisiana. It has now spread to many parts of the South. Singing, giving gifts, feasting, and rejoicing were all once pagan customs.

A Season to Celebrate

Christmas is more than a day in December. The season begins with Advent, from a Latin word meaning "coming." Advent starts on the fourth Sunday before Christmas. It ends on Christmas Day. Advent is a time of preparation. Christians learn about events leading up to Christ's birth each Sunday of Advent. Many people count off the weeks of Advent by displaying Advent wreaths with four candles. Each Sunday, one candle is lit. On Christmas Eve, a large central candle is lit to symbolize Christ. Just as the pagans lit candles to stand for the return of the sun, Christians light candles to stand for Christ. Advent calendars are another popular custom. Children count off the days until Christmas on a special calendar. A paper flap or window covers each day of the month. Behind each flap is a surprise, such as a piece of candy. Starting on December 1, children lift up a flap each day. They get surprises and count off the days until Christmas comes on December 25.

Christmas Day, December 25, is the date chosen to celebrate the birth of Christ. Some people may celebrate only this day, but the Christmas season actually lasts for 12 days. Epiphany is another

Firework displays are Christmas traditions in many places, including Italy, France, and Spain.

event to celebrate. Epiphany, the 12th day of Christmas, falls on January 6, which is 12 days after Christmas Eve. The word comes from the Latin word meaning "appearance." Epiphany was an early Roman festival that honored Christ's entrance into the world and the Magi's visit to Bethlehem. Today, Epiphany also marks the official close of the Christmas season. It is a time to take down the decorations and add another Christmas to our memories.

In America, the Christmas season starts with Santa's arrival at the big Thanksgiving Day parades and stretches through New Year's and Epiphany. There's plenty of time to celebrate!

Dressed in holiday red, children and their mother play with a Christmas present.

For many families, the best time is Christmas Eve. They invite relatives and friends to their homes for dinner. They may serve special foods that were part of the ethnic customs of their ancestors. (*Ethnic* means "of nations or groups.") Gaily wrapped gifts that have been waiting under the lighted tree are passed out to be opened. (Some gifts may be saved to unwrap on Christmas Day.) Children hang stockings for Santa Claus to fill during the night.

For many Christians, the highlight of Christmas is going to church on Christmas Eve. They listen to readings from the Bible and join in singing Christmas carols.

Other families wait until Christmas Day for feasting and gift opening. They may include church services and gathering with relatives and friends. And many American families carry on the tradition of celebrating both Christmas Eve and Christmas Day.

Christmas Comes to America

Christmas in America has changed over the years. The Puritans, who were among America's first settlers, came from England to seek religious freedom. They were very serious about their ideas of proper worship and refused to celebrate Christmas. They felt no day was more important than Sunday, the Sabbath, a day set aside for rest and worship. Besides, they said, Christ's birthdate was not actually known and birthday celebrations were pagan.

The Puritans of New England did not have the last word about Christmas, though. People from other countries also came to make America their home, bringing cherished traditions with them. After all, Christmas was centuries old! It was probably the Christmasloving immigrants from Germany and Ireland who finally convinced the New Englanders that Christmas could be a harmless, pleasant, and even religious, celebration after all. Charles Dickens's beloved 1843 novel, *A Christmas Carol*, helped break down the New England prejudice against Christmas, too. Tiny Tim showed Scrooge – and all people – how to keep Christmas in their hearts. Christmas celebrations spread as the nation grew. The first state to declare Christmas a legal holiday was Alabama, in 1836. The last was Oklahoma, in 1890.

Christmas in America is a mixture of customs and traditions from all the ethnic groups that have made America their home. Our Christmas heritage is a blend of customs from around the world and some that are distinctly American. The community Christmas tree is one. Elaborate outdoor lighting of buildings, trees, and lawns is another of our contributions. The United States has added some all-time favorites to the collection of Christmas songs, movies, and TV shows, too. And the Santa Claus of today is an American creation, even though his beginning goes way back in history.

Signs and Symbols of the Holiday

St. Nicholas Becomes Santa Claus

One of the best-loved figures of the Christmas season is Santa Claus. Who is this "right jolly old elf" who represents Christmas to so many?

To most modern Americans, St. Nicholas is just another name for Santa Claus. But to most Europeans, St. Nicholas is a tall, thin man dressed in bishop's robes who arrives on a white horse on St. Nicholas Day, December 6. The Santa many Americans know and love is an American creation, born in the 19th century. He is a combination of legends and history that go back many centuries.

In the fourth century, there lived a man named Nicholas, who was the bishop of Myra in Lycia. That ancient land is now part of Turkey. Nicholas was a kind and generous man, greatly loved by the people he served. He was fondly remembered after his death. In time, St. Nicholas became one of the most popular of all saints. He was the patron saint of Russia, and of sailors, students, and children. Little is known about the real St. Nicholas, but there are many legends and stories about his kindness, his love for children, and the miracles he brought about.

Legend has it that Nicholas enjoyed giving gifts in secret. As he walked through the streets, dressed in his official red cap and robe, he carried a bag filled with gifts. Any open window gave him the chance to slip a gift into a home without being discovered. Another story tells of the three daughters of a poor man who were unable to marry. This was because their father could not afford dowries (money or property that brides bring to their husbands). Father Nicholas secretly gave all three girls bags of gold so they could be married to respectable men.

The stories about St. Nicholas's secret gift giving inspired people from many other countries to do the same. The eve of the feast day of St. Nicholas became the day to enjoy this custom and to keep the St. Nicholas legend alive. Today, people in European countries leave shoes or stockings outside bedroom doors on December 5 in the hopes that St. Nicholas will secretly fill them with gifts. The feast day itself is observed on December 6 because St. Nicholas died on that day in A.D. 343. In those days, people celebrated an honored person's date of death rather than his or her date of birth.

Devotion to St. Nicholas spread. But with the Protestant Reformation, a religious movement of the 1500s, it became improper for Protestants to celebrate anything having to do with Catholic saints or pagan rituals. This movement gave birth to other Christian religions that split from the Catholic religion. Many Protestants began to consider Christmas an inappropriate holiday because it included nonreligious customs and Catholic rituals such as those associated with St. Nicholas. But St. Nicholas was far too popular to be done away with.

A few countries solved the problem simply by changing Nicholas's name. England turned him into Father Christmas. Germany called him Weihnachtsmann and France renamed him Père Noël. Germany also developed the Christkind, or Christ child, to become the gift giver. The Christkind tradition came with German immigrants to America, where his name was mispronounced and ended up as Kris Kringle.

People in Holland left St. Nicholas's name the same but changed the meaning of it into a nonreligious one. He became a jolly gift bringer like Father Christmas or Père Noël, but was still called by his old name. When the Dutch settled in New Amsterdam, which later became New York, they brought St. Nicholas (Sinterklaas) with them.

Since New England came from a Puritan beginning, saints and celebrations were rare in the earlier years. It was not until after the American Revolution (1775–1783, when the American colonies won their independence from England) that the Christmas customs of some of the immigrant groups began to spread.

The American writer Washington Irving described St. Nicholas in 1809 as a chubby little man with a jolly smile, who was driven by a

A 19th-century portrait of St. Nicholas, the bishop who rewarded his followers with gifts.

MERRY OLD SANTA CLAUS.

team of reindeer. His writing stirred up great interest in St. Nicholas. Irving's description of the jolly elf delighted Dr. Clement Moore of New York City. Moore later wrote a poem called *A Visit from St. Nicholas.*

The way we picture Santa (St. Nick) today comes from Dr. Moore's poem. He wrote it on December 24, 1822, for his six children. A family friend heard Dr. Moore read the poem to his children, and copied it down. The next Christmas, she sent it to a newspaper, where it was printed without the author's name. All were delighted with St. Nicholas as Dr. Moore saw him. This poem has become one of our best-loved Christmas traditions. People of all ages know the familiar words by heart: ''T'was the night before Christmas, when all through the house . . . ''

Dr. Moore's poem was the inspiration for Thomas Nast, the man who drew a picture of Santa Claus 44 years later. (By the 1860s, the old Dutch Sinterklaas was cheerfully mispronounced by Americans as ''Santa Claus.'') Thomas Nast drew Christmas cartoons for *Harper's Weekly.* In a famous 1866 cartoon, Nast showed Santa in his workshop with a sleigh and reindeer, stockings hung by the fireplace, and a Christmas tree nearby. He drew Santa as the ''right jolly old elf'' described in Dr. Moore's poem. His drawings were done in pen and ink – in black and white. In the 1920s, Santa Claus changed from black and white to color in ads for Coca-Cola. He had grown from the elf size of Dr. Moore and Thomas Nast's character to a fat, human-size Santa with rosy cheeks, bright red suit, buckled belt, and knee-high boots.

Thomas Nast's famous drawing of "the jolly old elf," which gave us our modern idea of what Santa Claus looks like

Christmas Trees and Evergreens

Whether it is chopped down in a forest, bought at an outdoor lot, or assembled out of a box, the Christmas tree joins Santa Claus as one of the world's best-loved holiday symbols.

Many people credit the German religious leader Martin Luther with the idea of decorating an evergreen tree at Christmastime. A legend describes how Martin Luther chopped down a tree in the forest, brought it home to his family, and decorated it with candles that stood for the stars shining over Bethlehem. But the use of the Christmas tree actually has beginnings long before the time of Luther.

Long before the birth of Christ, people celebrating the winter solstice brought evergreens into their homes to symbolize the green of the spring that would return with the sun. Egyptians brought palm branches into their homes. Romans trimmed trees with trinkets and toys during Saturnalia. The ancient Druid priests honored their god, Odin, by tying golden apples and other offerings onto tree branches. (The Druids were the priests and lawmakers of the Celts, a people of ancient Europe who worshiped many gods.)

When people accepted Christianity, they kept their winter rites but gradually changed them to honor Christ. Evergreens came to mean Christ bringing new life to the world after the long, dark days of winter. Martin Luther did much to make the Christmas tree popular in Germany in the 16th century.

A German carol, "O Tannenbaum," honored the Christmas tree. The trees then were table-size. Little cookies, red apples, and candles were originally the only decorations used. Beautiful as the candles were, they were a terrible fire hazard. In more cautious

German homes, the trees were lit only once, on Christmas Eve, when the parlor doors were opened and the children saw the trees for the first time. Buckets of water were lined up against the walls just in case a spark sent a tree up in flames.

Before the invention of light bulbs, Christmas trees were decorated with burning candles.

Every year a giant Christmas tree is put up in New York City's Rockefeller Center near the famous ice-skating rink.

The symbol of the Christmas tree spread to other countries as some Germans moved away and took their customs with them. The Christmas tree caught on in Switzerland and Austria. It became a familiar sight in Finland, Norway, Sweden, and Russia by the 19th century. In 1840, Princess Helene of Mecklenburg, Germany, went to France to marry the French king's eldest son. She brought the Christmas tree to France. In England, other German princesses became queens and kept up the tradition of the decorated tree. Generally, only royalty had the trees, but that changed when Queen Victoria reigned. She came to the throne in 1837, as a young woman of 18. She married her cousin, Prince Albert, a German. The royal wedding and the young couple's growing family enchanted the English people.

When Victoria and Albert decorated their tree with goodies, surrounded it with toys and dolls, and topped it with an angel, every middle-class family in England decided that it, too, must have a tree. Albert gave many decorated trees to schools, army barracks, and other places. Christmas trees suddenly appeared everywhere in England.

America's Christmas Trees

Legends say the first Christmas trees in America arrived with the Hessians, German soldiers hired by the British to fight in the American Revolution. We know for certain that the German colonists who settled in Pennsylvania decorated trees in the early 1820s. German immigrants introduced the trees in other parts of the country, too.

Only gradually did the custom spread among other Americans as well. In 1850, *Godey's Lady's Book,* the leading women's magazine in America, ran a picture of Queen Victoria's tree. Americans, with no royalty of their own, were enchanted with the young queen. To have a tree like Victoria's suddenly became the new fashion.

Americans were quick to accept the tradition of the Christmas tree. President Franklin Pierce put up the first White House Christmas tree in 1856. Three years after Thomas Edison invented electric light in 1879, the vice president of Edison's electric light company had the first Christmas tree lit by electricity. Only wealthy families could afford electric lights at first. In 1895, President Grover Cleveland delighted his children with electric lights on the White House tree. When strings of ready-made lights were invented, the tragic fires of candlelit trees became a thing of the past.

Not only has the Christmas tree been welcomed into American homes and churches, but it is playing a bigger part each year in community celebrations. The first outdoor Christmas tree with electric lights was set up in Pasadena, California, in 1909. New York City and Philadelphia, Pennsylvania, followed in 1912 and 1913. In 1920, Pasadena lit up a mile-long avenue called Christmas Tree Lane with more than 10,000 multicolored bulbs. Thousands of people, including visitors from abroad, enjoyed the display.

In 1923, President Calvin Coolidge lit the first outdoor tree at the White House. Since 1923, a tree has been brought to Washington each year from a different state. The national Christmas tree is lighted each year in a grand ceremony by the president. In 1954, President Dwight D. Eisenhower expanded the ceremony and invited delegates from 27 foreign embassies to participate in a "pageant of peace."

Many American cities have wonderful outdoor community trees. Rockefeller Center in New York City has a huge tree with special lighting every year. Northport, a shopping center near Seattle, Washington, set the record for displaying the tallest tree. In 1950, the center set up a 212-foot, 25-ton tree. Bethlehem, Pennsylvania, decorates its Hill-to-Hill Bridge with more than 150 spruces and 1,200 electric lights. Its span is crowned by a 60-foot tree made up of many smaller trees.

So fond are Americans of Christmas trees that they have a permanent symbol of Christmas. It is a giant sequoia, 287 feet high and more than 3,500 years old. Its trunk measures over 107 feet around. The tree stands in Kings Canyon National Park in California. It is the setting for many annual pilgrimages and Christmas programs.

The Manger Scene

One of the most important parts of Christmas in many Christian homes and churches is the manger scene, or crèche. The word *crèche* is the French word for manger or cradle. The custom probably comes from Greccio, the Italian town in which a famous crèche was set up by St. Francis of Assisi.

An angel, a shepherd, and one of the Magi attend Mary, Joseph, and the newborn Christ in a wooden crèche.

25

Poinsettias, the most popular Christmas flower

Fancy mangers of gold, silver, and jewels were built in churches all over Italy in the time of St. Francis. In 1223, St. Francis wanted to remind people that Christ was born in a humble stable. He recreated the Bethlehem Nativity scene with real people and animals on Christmas Eve in Greccio, Italy.

Inspired by St. Francis, artisans and craftsmen began to make miniature manger scenes for their homes, and the crèches spread all over Europe. Families made the manger figures from wood or clay. They made figures of Mary and Joseph, the baby Jesus, angels, shepherds, the Wise Men, and the animals.

The custom came to America in 1741 when the Moravians (people from a part of Czechoslovakia called Moravia) settled in Bethlehem, Pennsylvania. People from other countries came to America and brought their crèches. Crèches are now a familiar and important part of the American Christmas tradition.

Poinsettias

The most popular Christmas flower of all is the poinsettia. With its bright green leaves and its red or white petals shaped like stars, it is the flower of Christmas. This plant grows naturally in Mexico and Central America. The 17th-century friars in Mexico used poinsettias to decorate their Nativity celebrations.

America's first ambassador to Mexico, Dr. Joel Poinsett, introduced the plant to the United States in 1828. He was an amateur botanist (one who studies plants). He gave poinsettias to a number of friends. This winter-blooming plant must have 14 continuous hours of darkness every day from October 1 until about December 15 in order to bloom at Christmastime.

As with many Christmas customs, there is an old legend about the poinsettia. It tells of a poor little Mexican child who stopped by the roadside to pick some weeds to lay at the statue of the Virgin Mary. When he laid the weeds at the foot of the statue, they turned into beautiful flowers the color of fire and the shape of stars.

Mistletoe

Kissing under the green leaves and white berries of mistletoe is now a playful holiday custom. The ancient Druids thought the plant was holy. Over the centuries, feelings about mistletoe have gone from sacred to magical to playful. In early times, the plant was considered to be a cure for poisons. It was called "all-heal." But the custom of kissing suggests forgiveness. People hung mistletoe over their doors as a sign of welcome and friendship. Enemies who met under mistletoe would have to embrace and bury their grudges. In time, the kiss of peace has turned into a kiss in fun.

Holly

The bright green leaves and vivid red berries of the holly plant make it a favorite Christmas decoration. Since it kept its berries as well as its leaves throughout the winter, the pagans felt it must have magical powers. They believed wearing holly or decorating with it would promise the return of other plants after winter. Over time, holly came to stand for peace and joy. Superstitious people say holly tied to a bedpost will chase away nightmares. One thing is certain—holly berries are poisonous and will certainly make you sick!

This Christmas postcard carried holiday greetings many years ago.

Christmas Cards

It's always fun to check the mailbox at Christmastime. Friends from near and far send their greetings. Choosing and writing Christmas cards is a big part of getting ready for Christmas.

The Christmas card tradition started in England in 1843. Valentines and New Year's cards had been on the scene earlier, so the idea of sending good wishes to absent friends at Christmas caught on quickly.

Louis Prang, a German immigrant, is called "the father of the American Christmas card." The cards didn't really catch on in America until Prang started producing them in 1875. He invited artists to enter designs for cards. But competition from less costly foreign imports forced Prang to stop making cards in the 1890s.

When World War I cut off the supply of Christmas cards from Europe, American businessmen began making them again. Today, the selection is enormous. So many Christmas cards are sent that thousands of extra mail carriers are needed to deliver them all.

The Voices of Christmas

Soon after Thanksgiving, Christmas fills the air with its merry holiday music. People join together and sing carols up and down the streets, in shopping malls, and through schools, neighborhoods, and hospitals. Carols are heard everywhere. In England, *wassailing* is another word for caroling. Lighted windows signal carolers to stop and share their songs. Carolers are often offered refreshments for bringing good wishes and lovely music.

Many carols go far back in time. The United States has added its own to the world's collection of popular carols. Four of them are "It Came Upon a Midnight Clear," "O Little Town of Bethlehem," "We Three Kings of Orient Are," and "I Heard the Bells on Christmas Day."

The voice of Christmas is heard through more than songs. A holiday highlight for many families is watching a performance of *The Nutcracker* ballet. Others listen to Handel's *Messiah*. Many families read aloud holiday favorites such as *A Visit from St. Nicholas*, *A Christmas Carol*, Dr. Seuss's *How the Grinch Stole*

Singing Christmas carols at home was once a popular tradition.   31

Christmas, and other poems and stories. You probably have your own favorites to add to the list.

There are dozens of TV specials each Christmas. The heartwarming Christmas opera *Amahl and the Night Visitors* may be the world's best-known English opera, thanks to TV. Other specials entertain viewers with everything from the Peanuts gang to customs around the world. Holiday movies, too, are eagerly awaited traditions. *Miracle on 34th Street* has been a hit since 1947. *Holiday Inn* features Bing Crosby's singing of "White Christmas," which won an Oscar for best song in 1942 and turned into the biggest-selling record of all time.

These and others are cherished Christmas movies because their theme is the Christmas spirit, whether it be Santa Claus, gift giving, or the joy of family togetherness. You can be sure these movies will be popular for a long time to come!

Christmas in a Changing World

All Around America

The one thing we can always count on is change. People and their traditions are always on the move. Different ethnic populations in the United States have grown. This change has influenced holiday customs. In many parts of the United States, ethnic groups observe the Christmas customs of their ancestors.

Tiny Tim, the crippled boy in Charles Dickens's *A Christmas Carol*, expressed the true meaning of Christmas when he said "God bless us every one!"

Many black American families combine Christmas with an African-American holiday called Kwanza. This happy holiday lasts for seven days, from December 26 through January 1. It is based on the traditional African harvest festival. Each day families light a candle. They talk about one of the seven principles of black culture. The principles are creativity, faith, unity, responsibility, self-determination, cooperative economics, and purpose. There are gifts, music, feasting, and dancing.

Las Posadas is a popular tradition in parts of the American Southwest where large groups of Spanish- and Mexican-Americans live. *Posada* means inn or lodging, or a place to stay at night.

San Antonio, Texas, is one city where Las Posadas is celebrated. San Antonio is only 150 miles from Mexico. Over half of its people have Mexican or Spanish backgrounds. Many speak both English and Spanish. Their ethnic traditions unite the city in a joyous celebration.

San Antonio's River Walk is lit with thousands of *luminarias* (candles glowing from sand-filled bags). Tiny white lights sparkle from trees. Dancing and Mexican bands are part of a month-long celebration. Mexican-style Posadas are part of the festivities. The people form a parade and act out Mary and Joseph's search for a place to stay in Bethlehem. Two children carry statues of Mary and Joseph and lead the procession to "innkeepers" who say there is no room. When at last the children carrying Mary and Joseph find a place to stay, they place a tiny figure of the baby Jesus in a manger scene and the celebration begins.

There are treats, dances, and presents from a *piñata* – a hollow container that is stuffed with small presents and hung from the ceiling. All the children are blindfolded, spun around, and given a chance to swat the *piñata* with a stick. When it breaks apart, everyone scrambles for the gifts that fall out.

In a Las Posadas parade in California, two young people play Mary and Joseph looking for a room in an inn.

In New Mexico's Taos Pueblo, winter solstice and Christmas religious ceremonies are special outdoor events. Children dance to the piping of flutes while the aromas of stews, chilies, and bread pudding float through the pueblo. Nearby, a Taos horse ranch offers night rides in sleighs drawn by horses with flowing white manes and tails.

Ethnic celebrations in many other communities add spice to the season. In New Orleans, Père Noël cruises up the Mississippi past holiday bonfires. It's the official start of a month of Creole (French- and Spanish-American) festivities in the French Quarter.

In Holland, Michigan, toddlers in clogs (wooden shoes) practice Dutch ethnic dances for weeks before Christmas. Portuguese folk songs are sung in Fall River, Massachusetts. Holiday bakers roll out Moravian Christmas treats in Old Salem, North Carolina, and Bethlehem, Pennsylvania.

Around the same time as Christmas, Jewish families in Israel, the United States, and Canada observe their own religious holiday. It is the Jewish Feast of Lights, or Hanukkah. It lasts for eight days. Hanukkah falls sometime in November or December, depending on the Hebrew calendar. It celebrates how a small band of Jews in Jerusalem fought for religious freedom more than 2,000 years ago. They fought to regain the Jewish temple. They wanted to rebuild and purify their temple by lighting a holy lamp. They found only enough oil to keep the lamp burning for one day. But a miracle happened and the lamp remained lit for eight days. The miracle gave Jews great faith. Hanukkah menorahs (candelabra) are still lit by Jews everywhere to celebrate Hanukkah. Each evening, one additional candle is lighted until eight lighted candles stand together on the final evening. Children sing songs and have Hanukkah parties. They often receive gifts and money on each of the eight nights.

Americans all over the country are celebrating with the traditions of their ancestors. As our population grows and changes, Americans are sure to add new customs and find new ways to spread Christmas joy!

Christmas Is Big Business

Christmas is the time when store windows are crammed with gifts. Television, catalogs, and magazines tempt people with advertisements for things to put on Christmas lists. The boost in shopping at Christmastime can account for as much as one-third of a store's yearly sales. This may be as much as half of the year's total profits. Americans spend billions of dollars on gifts each Christmas.

A greenhouse full of healthy poinsettias, which have become a big holiday business

Toys, jewelry, and other gift items are some of the things that make Christmas a big-dollar season. Christmas-tree farming is a major forestry industry in the United States and Canada. Think about all the other things people buy at Christmas: cards, stamps, turkeys, gift wrap, party clothes, poinsettias, Christmas-tree lights, and more. All these things have become big industries.

Christmas items go on sale as early as Halloween. Still, the official opening of the holiday shopping season is traditionally the day after Thanksgiving. It has always been the busiest shopping day of the year. Many people have an extra day off at Thanksgiving. They look forward to Christmas shopping. Store owners look forward to jingling cash registers and big profits. America's high standard of living has produced the most lavish Christmas spending anywhere in the world as people buy gifts for family and friends.

Our Holiday Pace

Family schedules can begin to look like space shuttle prelaunch checklists as people rush to include extra holiday activities. There are plays and pageants, concerts and parties, and then shopping, baking, decorating, bill-paying, writing, and inviting. It's easy for adults and kids to get overwhelmed, tense, and tired. Sharing jobs, planning duties, and cutting out all but the most meaningful activities can help ease these holiday hassles.

For many, there's a big letdown when all the gifts are opened and the guests are gone. Feelings of disappointment are as normal after Christmas as excited feelings are beforehand. Planning new traditions to follow Christmas can ease the letdown. So can thinking of others. Inviting someone lonely, single, handicapped, or elderly to celebrate the holiday with you can be rewarding. Collecting food for a local food kitchen will brighten many holidays, including yours. "Presence" instead of presents is a gift money can't buy.

Keeping the Christmas Spirit

Though the traditions and celebrations last only a few weeks, Christmas is a holiday that is timeless. To spread peace and good-will–to be generous and kind–is the real spirit of Christmas. Christmas isn't merely a holiday or a season, but a state of mind. The Christmas spirit of sharing and caring is one to remember and practice all year. Merry Christmas!

Christmas Trivia

Did you ever wonder how fast Santa Claus has to move on Christmas in order to deliver all those presents? He has to visit two billion families in 24 hours. He and his reindeer must travel at about 70,000 miles an hour. Santa can stay at each house for only one-half of one ten-thousandth of a second!

Wise old saying: Christmas is a holiday when neither past nor future is as interesting as the present.

As late as 1870, Boston public school children went to school on Christmas Day. Christmas was outlawed in New England until the middle of the 19th century because of the continuing influence of the Puritans. A Massachusetts law of 1659 fined anyone who was caught celebrating Christmas.

At the time of the American Revolution, Christmas was not a national holiday. On Christmas night in 1776, George Washington crossed the Delaware. This action led to later victory in the Revolutionary War. The attack was unexpected by the Hessian soldiers (German soldiers hired to fight for the British). Why? They were busy celebrating their German-style Christmas!

There really is a North Pole—in fact, there are at least three of them with a post office! You'll find them in Colorado, zip code 80809; in Alaska, zip code 99705; and in New York, zip code 12947.

For genuine Yule postmarks, try Christmas, Florida 32709; Mistletoe, Kentucky 41351; Rudolph, Ohio 43462; Santa Claus, Indiana 47579; Snowflake, Virginia 24251; or Noel, Missouri 64854. Just bundle your Christmas cards into a large envelope and address it to the postmaster in one of these towns. He or she will then postmark them and send the cards on their way.

The United States issued its first Christmas stamp in 1962.

Many people abbreviate Christmas by writing *Xmas*. In Greek, *X* is the first letter of Christ's name. It was often used as a holy symbol.

Here's how to say ''Merry Christmas'' a dozen ways:
Joyeux Noël (France)
Frohliche Weihnachten (Germany)

According to Clement Moore's poem, St. Nick exclaimed, before he drove out of sight, "Happy Christmas to all, and to all a good night!"

Feliz Navidad (Mexico)
Glaedelig Jul (Norway)
Buon Natale (Italy)
Felices Pascuas (Spain)
Meri Kurisumasu (Japan)
Wesolych Swiat (Poland)
Prettige Kerstdagen (Holland)
S Roshestvom Khristovym (U.S.S.R.)
Kung Hei Shing Taan (China)
Kala Christ Ougena (Greece)

Originally, the family Christmas tree came from the forest. Today, most Christmas trees are raised on farms and plantations across the United States and Canada. These farms raise over 30 million trees a year!

A Visit from St. Nicholas by Clement C. Moore has been translated into many languages. There are yearly Christmas-season processions to Moore's grave in Trinity Cemetery in New York. Children sing carols and wait to hear a recitation of the poem. Dr. Moore wrote the poem in 1822 but did not admit he was the author until 1844. All his other writings were more serious. He was a little embarrassed to own up to the poem!

The story "Rudolph, the Red-Nosed Reindeer" was created in 1939 for Montgomery Ward and Company. It was just after the Great Depression. Ward's wanted something for their department store Santas to hand out. Their advertising writer, Robert May, came up with a simple tale about an outcast reindeer with a red nose. In 1949, May sent the story to a songwriter. Gene Autry, a cowboy-movie star, turned it into a hit song, which we hear every Christmas.

The ghost of Christmas past helps teach Ebenezer Scrooge to keep Christmas in his heart.

The real title on the book cover of Charles Dickens's *A Christmas Carol* is *A Christmas Carol in Prose, Being a Ghost Story of Christmas*. It sold over 6,000 copies the first day it came out in 1843 and remains a best-seller today. *A Christmas Carol* has been translated into almost every language.

Christmas in Sweden begins with St. Lucia Day on December 13. Lucia means "light." The oldest girl in the family wears a white dress with a red sash. This girl is called St. Lucia, and she reminds the Swedish people of a brave, kind-hearted girl named Lucia who lived in Italy in the second century. She was killed by the Romans for giving money and help to early Christians. She wears a crown of lingonberry leaves with five lighted candles on her head. Early in the morning, she wakes up the family with a song. For good luck, she serves them buns called *Lussekatter* (Lucia cats).

St. Nicholas Day, December 6, opens the Christmas season in Belgium, Germany, France, and Holland. Children in Holland watch St. Nicholas's arrival on television. From the Dutch port where he docks, he rides a white horse from house to house during the night. Children place their shoes by the chimney or their bedroom door for St. Nicholas to fill with gifts. They leave carrots, hay, or lumps of sugar for his horse.

For Further Reading

Enjoy the season's reading! These books have more information on Christmas customs and celebrations.

Barth, Edna. *Holly, Reindeer and Colored Lights*. New York: The Seabury Press, 1971.

Cuyler, Margery. *The All-Around Christmas Book*. New York: Holt, Rinehart and Winston, 1982.

Ebel, Holly. *Christmas in the Air*. Hopkins, Minn.: Hollyday Books, 1982.

Giblin, James Cross. *The Truth about Santa Claus*. New York: Thomas Y. Crowell, 1985.

Olliver, Jane. *The Doubleday Christmas Treasury*. Garden City, N.Y.: Doubleday & Company, Inc., 1986.

Patterson, Lillie. *Christmas Feasts and Festivals*. Champaign, Ill.: Garrard Publishing Company, 1968.

Index